About Mammals

Sobre los mamíferos

For the One who created mammals.
—*Genesis* 1:24

Para Aquél que creó a los mamíferos.
—*Génesis* 1:24

Published by
PEACHTREE PUBLISHERS
1700 Chattahoochee Avenue
Atlanta, Georgia 30318-2112
www.peachtree-online.com

Text © 1997, 1999, 2014 by Cathryn P. Sill
Illustrations © 1997, 1999, 2014 by John C. Sill
Spanish translation © 2014 by Peachtree Publishers

First bilingual edition published in hardcover and trade paperback in 2014

Also available in an English-language edition
ISBN 978-1-56145-757-1 (hardcover)
ISBN 978-1-56145-758-8 (paperback)

Spanish translation: Cristina de la Torre
Spanish-language copy editor: Cecilia Molinari

The publisher thanks René Valdés for his guidance with the Spanish animal names.

Illustrations painted in watercolor on archival quality 100% rag watercolor paper
Text and titles set in Novarese from Adobe Systems

Manufactured by Imago in China (bilingual hardcover) and by RR Donnelley & Sons in China (bilingual paperback)

10 9 8 7 6 5 4 3 2 1 (bilingual hardcover)
10 9 8 7 6 5 4 3 (bilingual paperback)

Library of Congress Cataloging-in-Publication Data

Sill, Cathryn P., 1953- author.
   About mammals : a guide for children = Sobre los mamíferos : una guía para niños / Cathryn Sill ; illustrated by John Sill ; translated by Cristina de la Torre.
      pages cm
   Parallel text in English and Spanish.
   ISBN 978-1-56145-815-8 (hardcover)
   ISBN 978-1-56145-800-4 (paperback)
   1. Mammals—Juvenile literature. I. Sill, John, illustrator. II. Torre, Cristina de la, translator. III. Sill, Cathryn P., 1953- About mammals. IV. Sill, Cathryn P., 1953- About mammals. Spanish. V. Title. VI. Title: Sobre los mamíferos.
   QL706.2.S54718 2014
   599—dc23
                                        2014002960

About Mammals
Sobre los mamíferos

A Guide for Children / Una guía para niños

Cathryn Sill
Illustrated by / *Ilustraciones de* John Sill
Translated by / *Traducción de* Cristina de la Torre

PEACHTREE
ATLANTA

Mammals have hair.

Los mamíferos tienen pelo.

They may have thick fur,

Pueden tener un pelaje denso,

PLATE 2 / LÁMINA 2
Muskox / buey almizclero

sharp quills,

púas afiladas

PLATE 3 / LÁMINA 3
North American Porcupine /
puercoespín norteamericano

or only a few stiff whiskers.

o solamente unos pocos bigotes tiesos.

PLATE 4 / LÁMINA 4
Walrus / *morsa*

Baby mammals drink milk from their mothers.

Las crías de los mamíferos se alimentan de la leche de su mamá.

PLATE 5 / LÁMINA 5
American Bison / *bisonte americano*

Some mammals are born helpless.

Algunos mamíferos nacen indefensos.

Others can move about on their own soon after they are born.

Otros echan a andar poco después de nacer.

PLATE 7 / LÁMINA 7
Elk / *ciervo canadiense*

Mammals may run,

Los mamíferos pueden correr,

PLATE 8 / LÁMINA 8
Pronghorn / berrendo

climb,

trepar,

swim,

nadar

PLATE 10 / LÁMINA 10
Blue Whale / ballena azul

or fly.

o volar.

PLATE 11 / LÁMINA 11
Big Brown Bat / *murciélago moreno*

Mammals eat meat,

Los mamíferos comen carne,

PLATE 12 / LÁMINA 12
Bobcat / *gato montés*

plants,

plantas

PLATE 13 / LÁMINA 13
American Pika / pica americana

or both.

o las dos cosas.

PLATE 14 / LÁMINA 14
American Black Bear / *oso negro*

They live in cold and icy places,

Habitan sitios fríos y glaciales,

PLATE 15 / LÁMINA 15
Arctic Fox / zorro polar

hot and dry deserts,

desiertos secos y calientes

PLATE 16 / LÁMINA 16
Black-tailed Jackrabbit /
liebre de California

or wet marshes.

o húmedos pantanos.

It is important to protect mammals
and the places where they live.

Es importante proteger a los mamíferos
y los lugares donde viven.

PLATE 18 / LÁMINA 18
Human / ser humano
Northern Raccoon / *mapache*
White-tailed Deer / *venado de cola blanca*
Eastern Gray Squirrel /
ardilla de las Carolinas

Afterword / Epílogo

PLATE 1

There are more than 5,000 species of mammals in the world. About 450 different kinds live in the United States and Canada. Hair is adapted to protect mammals according to the needs of each species. The coats of the Northern Raccoon grow thicker in winter to keep them warm and dry. Northern Raccoons are found in many different habitats across much of North America.

LÁMINA 1

Hay más de 5.000 especies de mamíferos en el mundo. En Estados Unidos y Canadá habitan alrededor de 450 de ellas. El pelaje de los mamíferos se adapta para protegerlos de acuerdo con las necesidades de cada especie. El del mapache se hace más denso durante el invierno para mantenerlos secos y abrigados. Los mapaches se encuentran en muchos hábitats distintos en casi toda América del Norte.

PLATE 2

Hair protects mammals in different kinds of weather. It also helps keep the animal's skin from being injured or sunburned. Many mammals have more than one kind of hair. The hair most easily seen is called "guard hair." Beneath the guard hair is a layer called "underfur." Muskoxen have a thick outer coat of long guard hairs and a dense undercoat that keep them warm in frigid temperatures. Muskoxen live in the cold Arctic region.

LÁMINA 2

El pelaje protege a los mamíferos en diferentes climas. También sirve para evitar heridas en la piel o quemaduras del sol. Muchos mamíferos tienen más de un tipo de pelaje. El pelaje exterior más visible se conoce como "pelo guardián". El que está debajo de este es el llamado "pelo suave". El pelo guardián de los bueyes almizcleros es largo y abundante mientras que la densa capa interior los protege de las temperaturas frígidas. Los bueyes almizcleros habitan las gélidas regiones árticas.

PLATE 3

Some mammals have thick, stiff guard hairs on parts of their bodies. North American Porcupines have sharp quills on their backs and tails. The quills are loosely attached and will come off and stick into an enemy's body. North American Porcupines live in the northern and western parts of North America.

LÁMINA 3

Algunos mamíferos tienen tiesos pelos guardianes en distintas partes del cuerpo. Los puercoespines norteamericanos poseen afiladas púas en el lomo y la cola. Las púas están sujetas muy levemente de modo que se desprenden con facilidad para clavarse en el cuerpo de un enemigo. Los puercoespines norteamericanos habitan zonas del norte y del oeste de América del Norte.

PLATE 4

Whiskers are a special kind of hair that helps mammals learn information about their surroundings. Some marine mammals have only a few coarse whiskers. Walruses use their sensitive, bristly whiskers to find food on the ocean floor. They eat snails, clams, crabs, and shrimp. Walruses live in the Arctic Ocean and some northern parts of the Pacific and Atlantic Oceans.

LÁMINA 4

Los bigotes son un tipo especial de pelo que los mamíferos usan para recolectar información de su entorno. Algunos mamíferos marinos tienen solamente unos pocos pelos hirsutos. Las morsas usan sus sensibles y erizados bigotes para buscar alimentos en el fondo del mar. Comen caracoles, almejas, cangrejos y camarones. Las morsas habitan el océano Ártico y algunas zonas norteñas del Pacífico y del Atlántico.

PLATE 5

Mammals get their name from the special mammary glands that make milk for their young. American Bison babies drink milk from their mothers for about seven months. American Bison (also called "American Buffalo") were nearly hunted to extinction in the late 1800s. Laws now protect them and their numbers are slowly increasing. American Bison are the largest land animals in North America. They live in central and western United States and Canada.

LÁMINA 5

Los mamíferos derivan su nombre de unas glándulas mamarias especiales que elaboran la leche para sus crías. Las crías de los bisontes americanos se alimentan de la leche de su madre alrededor de siete meses. Los bisontes americanos (también llamados búfalos americanos) casi desaparecieron a fines del siglo XIX debido al exceso de caza. Hoy día están protegidos por la ley y su número aumenta lentamente. Los bisontes americanos son los animales terrestres más grandes de América del Norte. Habitan zonas del centro y del oeste de Estados Unidos y Canadá.

PLATE 6

Mother mammals usually take good care of their babies. They feed, groom, and protect them until they are able to live on their own. White-footed Deermice are born blind and hairless. Their eyes open when they are about two weeks old. The babies are weaned at around three weeks. By the time they are ten or eleven weeks old, they have grown to adult size. White-footed Deermice live throughout most of the eastern United States. They also live in parts of Canada and Mexico.

LÁMINA 6

Las mamás de los mamíferos suelen cuidar muy bien de sus crías. Las alimentan, las limpian y las protegen hasta que son capaces de sobrevivir por su cuenta. Los ratones ciervos patiblancos nacen ciegos y sin pelo. No abren los ojos hasta las dos semanas y lactan hasta las tres semanas más o menos. A las diez u once semanas ya han alcanzado su tamaño adulto. Los ratones ciervos patiblancos habitan el este de Estados Unidos y algunas zonas de Canadá y México.

PLATE 7

Grazing mammal babies must be able to travel along as their mothers search for food. The young animals must be able to run very fast soon after birth to avoid danger from predators. Elk (also called "Wapiti") babies can stand up about twenty minutes after they are born. Elk used to be common over most of North America, but hunting caused them to disappear from eastern North America. They have been successfully reestablished in several places where they used to live.

LÁMINA 7

Las crías de los animales que pastan deben poder desplazarse con su mamá en busca de alimentos. Y deben ser capaces de correr a gran velocidad desde que nacen para escapar de los predadores. Las crías de los ciervos canadienses (también llamados wapitís) suelen levantarse a los veinte minutos de nacidas. Los ciervos canadienses eran muy comunes en casi toda América del Norte, pero la caza los eliminó del este del continente. Se ha logrado restablecerlos en varios de sus antiguos hábitats.

PLATE 8

Most land mammals walk or run on all four legs. Pronghorns must be able to run fast to escape from danger since they live in open areas without many hiding places. They can run over 50 miles per hour (80 km/h) for several miles. Pronghorns are the fastest mammals in North America. They live in western and central North America.

LÁMINA 8

La mayoría de los mamíferos de tierra caminan o corren en cuatro patas. Los berrendos deben correr a grandes velocidades para escapar del peligro ya que habitan campos abiertos con pocos sitios donde esconderse. Los berrendos son los mamíferos más veloces de América del Norte. Son capaces de correr por varias millas a velocidades hasta de 50 millas por hora (80 km/h). Habitan zonas del oeste y del centro de América del Norte.

PLATE 9

Animals that climb must be able to hold on to keep from falling. Squirrels have sharp claws that help them grasp trunks and branches and allow them to make their way easily through trees. American Red Squirrels are small, noisy tree squirrels that stay safe from predators by moving quickly. They live in forests in parts of the United States and Canada.

LÁMINA 9

Los animales que trepan deben poder agarrarse bien para no caerse. Las ardillas tienen garras afiladas que les sirven para asir las ramas y los troncos, y así circular fácilmente por entre los árboles. Las pequeñas y chillonas ardillas rojas americanas escapan de sus predadores moviéndose con gran rapidez. Habitan los bosques de partes de Estados Unidos y Canadá.

PLATE 10

Mammals that live in the water all of the time use their flippers to steer and their tails to push themselves as they swim. Blue Whales are the largest animals that have ever lived on Earth. They swim in all the oceans of the world.

LÁMINA 10

Los mamíferos que viven en el agua todo el tiempo usan las aletas para navegar y las colas para impulsarse nadando. Las ballenas azules son los animales más grandes que jamás han habitado la Tierra. Se encuentran en todos los océanos del mundo.

PLATE 11

While some mammals can glide from tree to tree, bats are the only ones that truly fly. Big Brown Bats are one of the fastest bats. They can fly at speeds up to 40 miles per hour (64 km/h). Big Brown Bats eat flying insects, including beetles, moths, flies, and wasps. They live in North America, Central America, the northern part of South America, and the Caribbean Islands.

LÁMINA 11

Aunque hay mamíferos que pueden transitar entre los árboles, los únicos que realmente vuelan son los murciélagos. Los murciélagos morenos alcanzan velocidades hasta de 40 millas por hora (64 km/h) en el aire. Se alimentan de insectos voladores tales como escarabajos, polillas, moscas y avispas. Habitan América del Norte, Central y partes de América del Sur y las islas del Caribe.

PLATE 12

Animals that eat meat are called "carnivores." Some mammals, such as wild cats, eat only meat. Although Bobcats can kill animals larger than themselves, they hunt mainly rabbits, squirrels, and mice. Bobcats live throughout most of North America.

LÁMINA 12

Los animales que se alimentan de carne se llaman "carnívoros". Algunos mamíferos, por ejemplo los gatos salvajes, comen solamente carne. Los gatos monteses cazan principalmente conejos, ardillas y ratones, aunque son capaces de matar animales de mayor tamaño que ellos. Los gatos monteses se extienden por casi toda América del Norte.

PLATE 13

Animals that eat plants are called "herbivores." Some plant eaters store food for winter. In midsummer, American Pikas begin to gather plants and pile them into stacks to dry in the sun. They often tuck the dried plants under a rock or log to protect them from the weather. When snow covers the ground, they move through tunnels they have built to find their "haystacks." American Pikas live in the mountains of western North America.

LÁMINA 13

Los animales que se alimentan de plantas se llaman "herbívoros". Algunos de ellos almacenan alimentos para el invierno. A mediados del verano las picas americanas comienzan a recoger plantas y amontonarlas para que se sequen al sol. A menudo meten las plantas ya secas bajo una piedra o un tronco para protegerlas del mal tiempo. Cuando el suelo está cubierto de nieve, se mueven a través de túneles que han construido en busca de sus "pajares". Las picas americanas habitan las montañas del oeste de América del Norte.

PLATE 14

Animals that eat meat and plants are called "omnivores." Most kinds of bears are omnivores. American Black Bears will eat many different things, including roots, berries, insects, and small mammals. They are able to live in forests, swamps, and tundra. American Black Bears are the most common bear in North America. They live in Canada, the United States, and northern Mexico.

LÁMINA 14

Los animales que se alimentan de carne y de plantas se llaman "omnívoros". Casi todos los osos son omnívoros. Los osos negros comen una gran variedad de cosas, incluyendo raíces, bayas, insectos y pequeños mamíferos. También pueden sobrevivir en diversos hábitats, como bosques, pantanos y tundras. Los osos negros son los osos más comunes de América del Norte. Habitan Canadá, Estados Unidos y el norte de México.

PLATE 15

Many animals migrate from cold areas when winter comes. Those that stay are protected from the cold by thick layers of fat or dense fur coats. Arctic Foxes have white winter coats that change to brown in summer. This camouflage or protective coloration allows them to hide from both predators and prey. They have fur on their paws so they can walk on ice and snow. Arctic Foxes live throughout the entire Arctic Tundra.

LÁMINA 15

Muchos animales migran de zonas gélidas al llegar el invierno. Los que se quedan tienen gruesas capas de grasa o denso pelaje para protegerse del frío. Los zorros polares son blancos en invierno pero se tornan pardos durante el verano. Este camuflaje, o coloración protectora, les permite pasar inadvertidos tanto de sus predadores como de sus presas. Además tienen pelo en las patas para poder andar sobre el hielo y la nieve. Los zorros polares se extienden por toda la tundra ártica.

PLATE 16

Desert mammals have special ways of surviving in their hot, dry habitat. Black-tailed Jackrabbits have large ears that carry the heat away from their bodies. Their excellent hearing helps them avoid predators. Jackrabbits are hares, not rabbits. Hares are usually larger than rabbits and have larger back legs and feet. Jackrabbits live in central and western North America.

LÁMINA 16

Los mamíferos del desierto tienen modos especiales de sobrevivir en ese entorno caliente y seco. Las grandes orejas de las liebres de California les sirven para eliminar el calor del cuerpo. Y su excelente sentido del oído les avisa de la presencia de predadores. Aunque parecidas a los conejos, las liebres son de mayor tamaño que ellos y tienen las patas traseras mucho más grandes. Habitan zonas del centro y del oeste de América del Norte.

PLATE 17

Many mammals are able to find food and shelter in marshes or other types of wetlands. Common Muskrats build domed houses in water using marsh vegetation. Their tails, which are flattened from side to side, help guide them as they swim. Common Muskrats live in most of Canada and the United States.

LÁMINA 17

Muchos mamíferos encuentran alimento y refugio en los pantanos o en otros tipos de humedales. Las ratas almizcleras construyen madrigueras abovedadas en el agua usando la vegetación de las ciénagas. Su cola, plana de lado a lado, las ayuda a navegar mientras nadan. Las ratas almizcleras viven en casi todas partes de Estados Unidos y Canadá.

PLATE 18

One of the greatest dangers to mammals and other wildlife is habitat destruction. When we protect the environment, we benefit mammals as well as whole communities of different animals by providing places where they can find space, shelter, food, and water.

Can you find the animal in this picture that is not a mammal?

LÁMINA 18

Uno de los peligros más graves para los mamíferos y otros animales salvajes es la destrucción de su hábitat. Cuando protegemos el medio ambiente beneficiamos tanto a los mamíferos como a otras comunidades de diferentes animales al proveerles sitios con suficiente espacio donde encontrar refugios, alimentos y agua.

En la ilustración, ¿puedes encontrar el animal que no es un mamífero?

GLOSSARY

Glide—to move smoothly without effort
Graze—to feed on growing grass
Groom—to clean fur or skin
Habitat—the place where animals and plants live
Marine Mammal—a mammal that spends all or part of its life in the sea
Predator—an animal that lives by hunting and eating other animals
Prey—an animal that is hunted and eaten by a predator
Species—a group of animals or plants that are alike in many ways
Wean—to help a nursing baby learn to find other food

GLOSARIO

Abovedada: curvada
Especie: grupo de animales o plantas que son semejantes en muchos aspectos
Hábitat: sitio donde viven animales y plantas
Lactar: cuando una cría se alimenta de la leche materna
Madrigueras: refugios
Mamífero marino: mamífero que pasa toda o parte de su vida en el mar
Predador: animal que se alimenta de otros animales
Presa: animal que es cazado y devorado por un predador

BIBLIOGRAPHY

BOOKS

Eyewitness Books: Mammal by Steve Parker (Dorling Kindersley)
Kaufman Focus Guides: Mammal by Nora Bowers, Rick Bowers, and Kenn Kaufman (Houghton Mifflin Company)
Peterson First Guides: Mammals by Peter Alden (Houghton Mifflin Company)

WEBSITES

http://kids.sandiegozoo.org/animals/mammals
http://www.enchantedlearning.com/subjects/mammals/
http://www.arkive.org/mammals/

ABOUT... SERIES

ISBN 978-1-56145-234-7 HC
ISBN 978-1-56145-312-2 PB

ISBN 978-1-56145-038-1 HC
ISBN 978-1-56145-364-1 PB

ISBN 978-1-56145-688-8 HC
ISBN 978-1-56145-699-4 PB

ISBN 978-1-56145-301-6 HC
ISBN 978-1-56145-405-1 PB

ISBN 978-1-56145-256-9 HC
ISBN 978-1-56145-335-1 PB

ISBN 978-1-56145-588-1 HC

ISBN 978-1-56145-207-1 HC
ISBN 978-1-56145-232-3 PB

ISBN 978-1-56145-757-1 HC
ISBN 978-1-56145-758-8 PB

ISBN 978-1-56145-358-0 HC
ISBN 978-1-56145-407-5 PB

ISBN 978-1-56145-331-3 HC
ISBN 978-1-56145-406-8 PB

ISBN 978-1-56145-795-3 HC

ISBN 978-1-56145-743-4 HC
ISBN 978-1-56145-741-0 PB

ISBN 978-1-56145-536-2 HC
ISBN 978-1-56145-811-0 PB

ISBN 978-1-56145-183-8 HC
ISBN 978-1-56145-233-0 PB

ISBN 978-1-56145-454-9 HC

**ALSO AVAILABLE
IN BILINGUAL EDITION**

- About Birds / Sobre los pájaros
  ISBN 978-1-56145-783-0 PB
- About Mammals / Sobre los mamíferos
  ISBN 978-1-56145-800-4 PB

ABOUT HABITATS SERIES

ISBN 978-1-56145-641-3 HC
ISBN 978-1-56145-636-9 PB

ISBN 978-1-56145-734-2 HC

ISBN 978-1-56145-559-1 HC

ISBN 978-1-56145-469-3 HC
ISBN 978-1-56145-731-1 PB

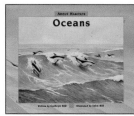

ISBN 978-1-56145-618-5 HC

ISBN 978-1-56145-432-7 HC
ISBN 978-1-56145-689-5 PB

THE SILLS

Cathryn Sill, a graduate of Western Carolina University, was an elementary school teacher for thirty years.

John Sill is a prize-winning and widely published wildlife artist. A native of North Carolina, he holds a B.S. in wildlife biology from North Carolina State University.

The Sills have published twenty-one books about nature for children. They live in North Carolina.

Cathryn Sill, graduada de Western Carolina University, fue maestra de escuela primaria durante treinta años.

John Sill es un pintor de vida silvestre que ha publicado ampliamente y merecido diversos galardones. Nacido en Carolina del Norte, es diplomado en biología de vida silvestre por North Carolina State University.

Los Sill, que han colaborado en vientiún libros para niños sobre la naturaleza, viven en Carolina del Norte.